How to Crochet a Baby Blanket for Beginners

Simple Baby Blanket Crochet Patterns And Tutorials

Table of Content

Introduction

New baby on the way? A crocheted baby blanket makes a great gift, and these patterns make it simple for even new crocheters to create something beautiful.

Most patterns in this list use basic stitches, while a few have simple but new-to-you stitch patterns. Some you can work on in small pieces over time and others are so easy you can make them in a single day.

Whether you make a blanket for a shower gift or as you wait for your little one to arrive, these patterns are sure to keep baby all snuggly.

Fleece-Lined Hexagon Baby Blanket

If you get tired or frustrated with creating a blanket in rows and turning the whole things around, you're going to love this pattern. The Hudson blanket is just a bunch of different hexagons in different colors and they're each made separately. It's much faster and easier to whip up a stack of smaller shapes than to work on a large blanket. Once all the hexies were made, all I had to do was seam them all together. That step does take a bit longer, but it's an easy task to do and goes by quickly.

HOW TO MAKE
Materials:
- 8 skeins of #4 worsted weight yarn – I used 2 each in I Love This Yarn in Greybeard (Color

A), Turquoise (Color B), White (Color C) and Aegean Stripe (Color D) for the border.

- 1,5 yards of no-pill fleece
- 4.00mm crochet hook*
- a rotary cutter with skip stitch blades*
- tapestry needle

Abbreviations:

- ch – chain
- SC – single crochet
- DC – double crochet
- sl – slip stitch

Pattern Notes:

Skill level: Beginner/intermediate

Sizing: 40 x 40 inches

Gauge: 4S x 2R per inch

Full Hexagon:

Make 20 of these in Color A (Greybeard), 16 in Color B (Turquoise) and 16 in Color C (White).

Round 1: Start with a magic loop and secure it with a slip stitch. Chain 2 (count as DC). Work 1 DC into the magic loop. Chain 2 again. *DC 2, chain 2* five more times into the magic loop. You should have 6 sets of DC and 5 chain-2 spaces now. Slip stitch to the top of the ch 2 to finish the round. Then, pull the loop closed.

Round 2: Ch 2, DC. (DC, ch 2, DC) into the chain-2

space. *DC 2, [DC, ch2, DC]* repeat around and slip stitch to the top of the beginning ch 2.

Round 3: Chain 2, DC 2. (DC, ch 2, DC) into the chain-2 space. *DC 4, [DC, ch2, DC]* repeat around to the last ch-2 space. DC 1 and slip stitch to the top of the beginning ch 2. (6 DC per side).

Round 4: Chain 2, DC 3. (DC, ch 2, DC) into the chain-2 space. *DC 6, [DC, ch2, DC]* repeat around to the last ch-2 space. DC 2 and slip stitch to the top of the beginning ch 2. (8 DC per side).

Round 5: Chain 2, DC 4. (DC, ch 2, DC) into the chain-2 space. *DC 8, [DC, ch2, DC]* repeat around to the last ch-2 space. DC 3 and slip stitch to the top of the beginning ch 2. (10 DC per side).

Round 6: Chain 2, DC 5. (DC, ch 2, DC) into the chain-2 space. *DC 10, [DC, ch2, DC]* repeat around to the last ch-2 space. DC 4 and slip stitch to the top of the beginning ch 2. (12 DC per side).

Half Hexagons:
Make 4 in Color B (Turquoise) and 4 in Color C (White)

 Round 1: Start with a magic loop and secure it with a slip stitch. Chain 2 (count as DC). Work 1 DC. Ch 2, *DC 2, ch 2* twice more. Pull the tail ends to close the loop. You should have 3 sets of DC and 2 chain-2 spaces now.

Round 2: Chain 2, turn. *DC 2, then (DC, ch 2, DC) into the ch-2 space* twice. DC 2, increase. (4 DCs per side)

Round 3: Chain 2, turn. .*DC 4, then (DC, ch 2, DC) into the ch-2 space* twice. DC 3, increase. (6 DCs per side)

Round 4: Chain 2, turn. *DC 6, then (DC, ch 2, DC) into the ch-2 space* twice. DC 4, increase. (8 DCs per side)

Round 5: Chain 2, turn. *DC 8, then (DC, ch 2, DC) into the ch-2 space* twice. DC 5, increase. (10 DCs per side)

Round 6: Chain 2, turn. .*DC 10, then (DC, ch 2, DC) into the ch-2 space* twice. DC 6, increase. (12 DCs)

Seaming It All Together

Once you have all of the hexagons, it's time to arrange them in the pattern you want and sew it all together. For my blanket, this is the pattern I followed.

ROW 1: Gray, turquoise, white, gray, turquoise, white, gray
ROW 2: Turquoise (half), white, gray, turquoise, white, gray, turquoise, white (half)

Repeat these rows three more times to finish. Then, thread your tapestry needle with a long length of yarn and use the invisible seam method to attach each hexagon to the one next to it. I did all of the short sides first so that I had long rows of hexagon strip, and then I went back and sewed the rows together. It's sort of like piecing together a quilt.

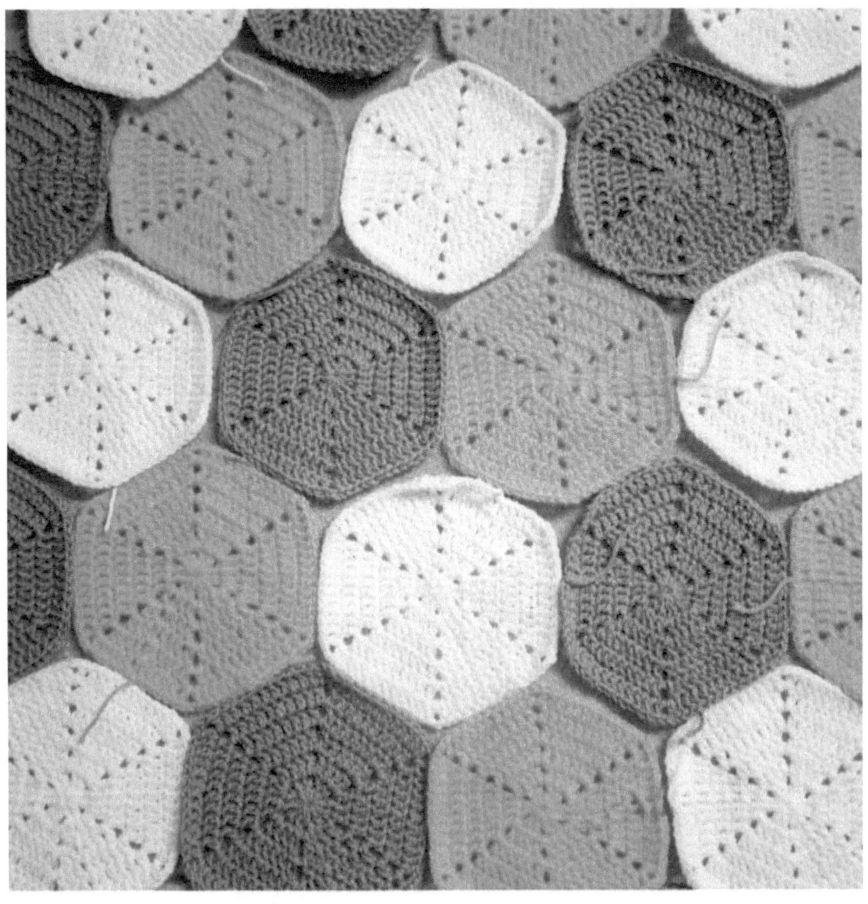

It does take a while to do, but it's easy and you just need to spend some time on it. I hate seaming, but the effect is so nice that I really do think it's worth it! Weave the tail ends in as best you can. Don't worry too much about it though; as long as they don't show on the front, they'll either be covered by the fleece or worked into the border.

Blocking, Adding Fleece, and the Border

For me, the best part of this hexagon baby blanket (and most of the baby blankets I make) is the fleece lining. It adds weight to the blanket and stays on the baby when they move around, and it has a comforting presence. It also makes the blanket much softer and warmer. However, if you don't want to add the fleece, you can go ahead and skip to the section on adding the border.

First, blocking.
Before adding the fleece, lightly block the blanket so that all the hexagons are as they should be. They might have gotten a little out of shape if you sewed them too tightly together or a little unevenly. But a simple blocking will fix that and make sure that two of the edges are straight. I have blocking mats now that help me align the edge but if you don't, a couple of towels works well too.

Prepping the fleece

On a large surface, lay out your fleece and smoothe it out. Then, lay your blanket on top of it, matching up two of the edges. Smoothe it out and make sure it all lines up. Using a pair of sharp scissors, cut the fleece to a little bigger than the size of the blanket. Make sure to not to cut the yarn!

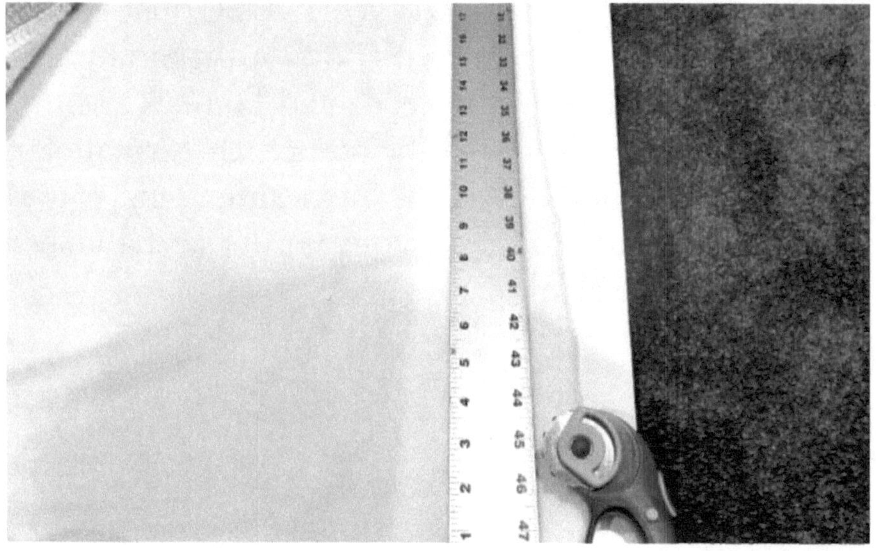

Remove the blanket for now and let's just work with the fleece. This is where we'll make the holes into the edges of the fleece so that we can insert our hook into it to crochet the fleece and blanket together. Put a cutting mat or a piece of cardboard under the edge of the fleece to protect your surface and bring a ruler about a quarter inch away from the edge of the fleece. Then, run your skip stitch down the side of the ruler. The skip stitch is the same as a rotary blade, but it perforates as it cuts into the fleece, rather than cutting a straight line. Work down all four sides of the fleece so that you have small slits along each side.

Now let's secure the fleece to the blanket!

Bring the blanket back to the fleece and line up the first corner. With your crochet hook, attach yarn in the border color (Color D). Work 1 SC just in the corner of the blanket. Then, SC down the side going through the spaces in the crocheted blanket and the slits made in the fleece. At the corner, ch 1, rotate the blanket and work down the next side. This round gives you the first round of your border and attaches the fleece to the blanket.

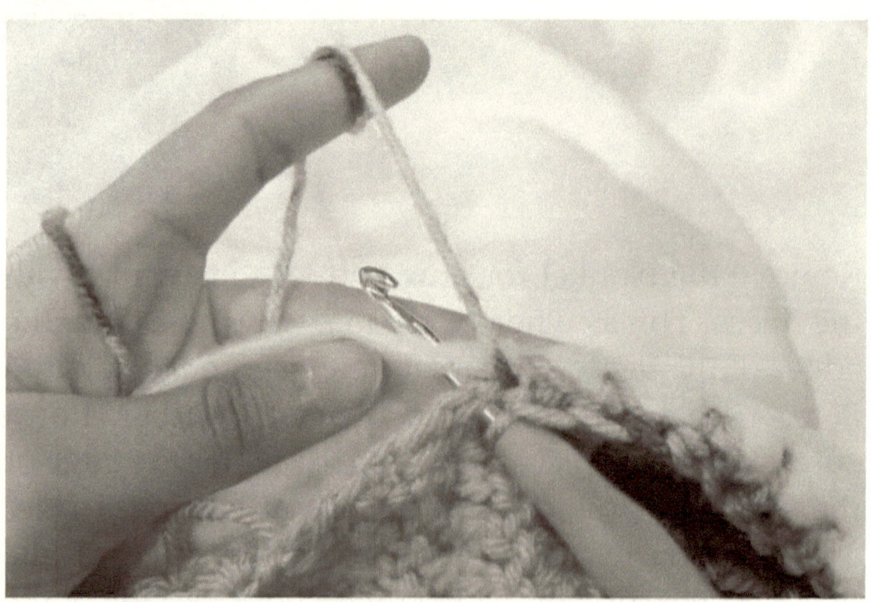

Work one more round of SC around the blanket, making sure to ch 1 before turning the corners.

The Bobble Border

1. Chain 5 at the corner of the blanket.
2. Into the 2nd chain from the hook, work 1 HDC but only pull the yarn through the first two loops. You'll have two loops remaining on the hook. Work 3 more HDC the same way, being sure to only pull through the first two loops each time.
3. You should now have 5 loops on the hook. YO, and pull through all 5 loops.
4. Slip stitch into the same space to finish off the bobble.
5. Slip stitch twice into the next two chain spaces.
6. SC into each of the next two SC spaces. Repeat steps 1-6 all around the blanket and bind off.

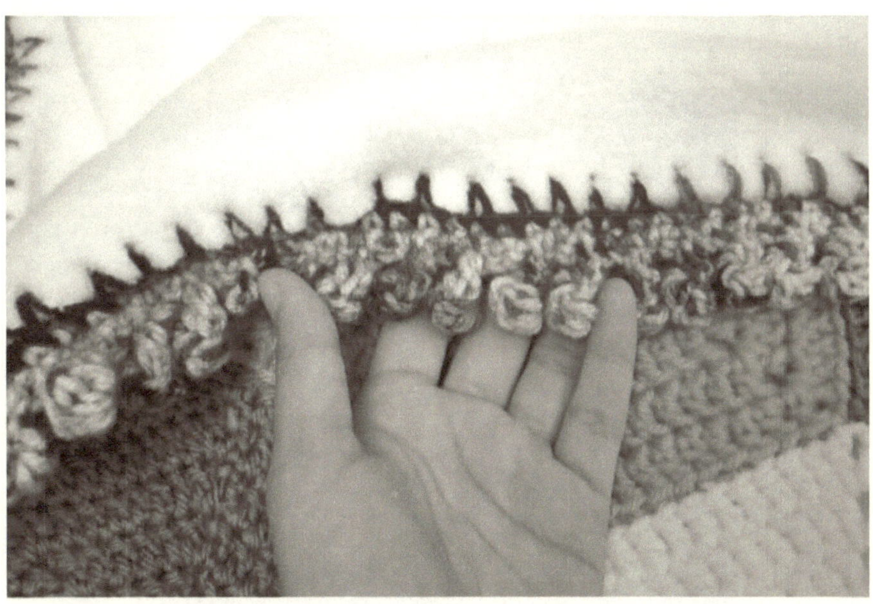

And you're done!

Weave in any loose ends and trim the excess yarn, and you're done with the Hudson blanket!

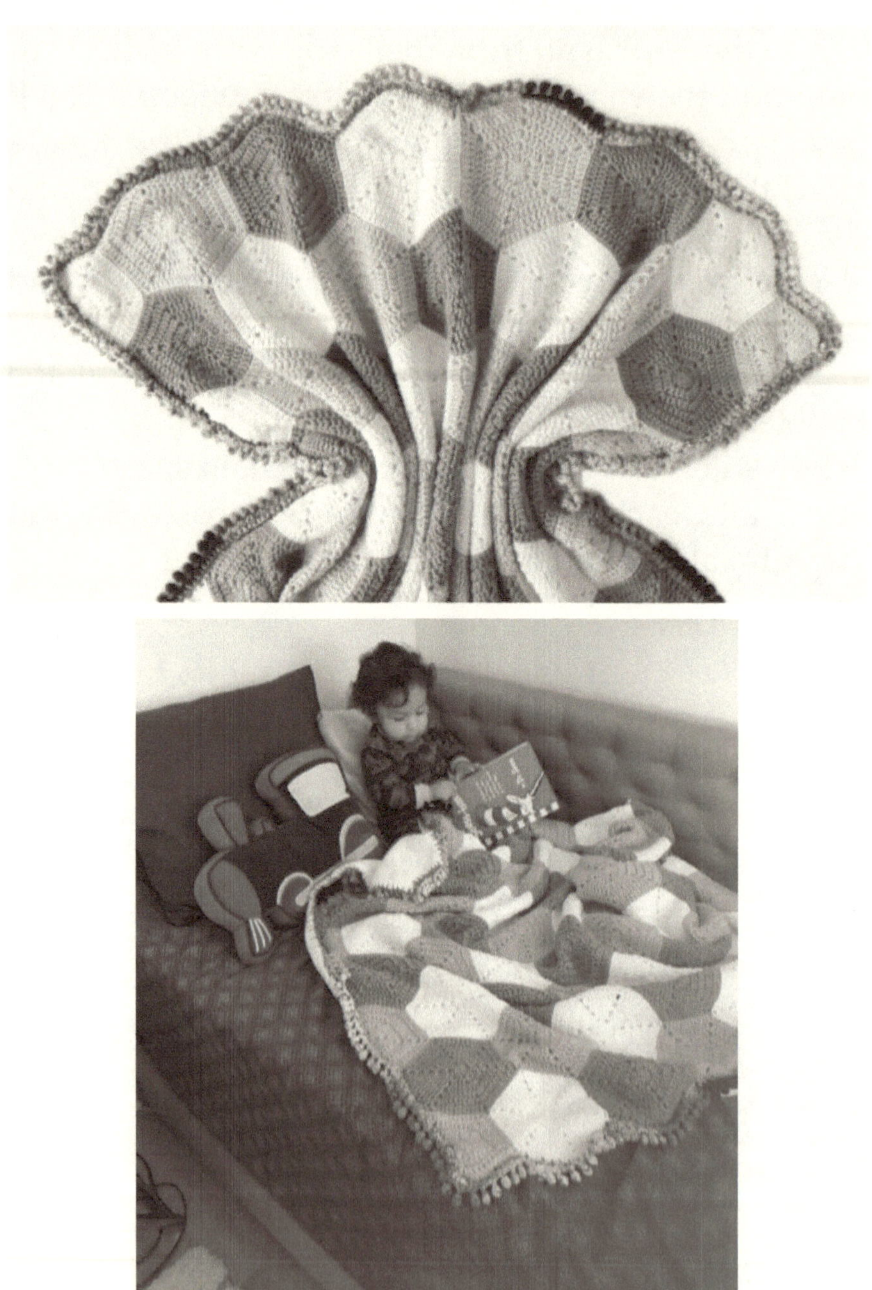

Gender-Neutral Crochet Baby Blanket

This colorful crocheted baby blanket features ripples of double crochet in bold stripes. It's a fresh take on a classic, and one that any parent would love to wrap their baby in. Plus, when you use a mix of bright and pastel colors, it can work from newborn through toddler years and beyond!

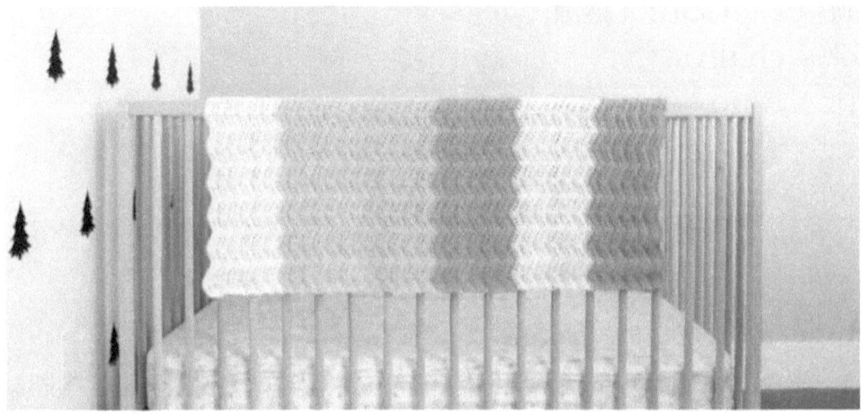

HOW TO MAKE
Measurements: 31" x 39" (See pattern notes to adjust size.)

Supplies:
• 1080 yds Lion Brand Baby Soft (DK/yarn symbol "3" – 459 yds, 5 oz)
 – Color A: Pastel Yellow (approx. 180 yds)
 – Color B: Lemon Drop (approx. 180 yds)
 – Color C: Creamsicle (approx. 180 yds)
 – Color D: Apricot (approx. 180 yds)
 – Color E: Mint (approx. 180 yds)

– Color F: Teal (approx. 180 yds)
• Tapestry needle
• Size H [5.0 mm] crochet hook

Gauge:

17 dc = 4″, slightly over 7 rows = 4″ worked in double crochet ripple pattern

Abbreviations and Glossary:

ch – chain
dc – double crochet
dc3tog – double crochet three together
tch – turning chain
yo – yarn over

Overall Pattern Notes:

• You can easily adjust the width of this blanket. Pattern is worked in multiples of 10 stitches + 1, plus 3 for the foundation chain. For example, the pattern as written is (10 x 12) = 120 ch, plus 1, which equals 121, plus three for the foundation chain for a total of 124 chains to begin. A larger blanket might be something like (10 x 20) = 200 ch, plus 1, which equals 201, plus three for the foundation chain for a total of 204 chains to begin.

• To switch colors, use the color of the upcoming row to complete the final yo of the row you're finishing. Proceed with new color in the next row. (See photo below.)

• Crochet over yarn tails as you switch colors and you will end up with very few, if any, ends to weave in at the end! (See photo below.)

complete last double crochet of row with new color   work over yarn tails

Foundation Row: Using Color A, ch 124.

Row 1: Skip first 3 ch (counts as 1 dc), 1 dc in fourth ch, *1 dc in each of next 3 ch, dc3tog over next 3 ch, 1 dc in each of next 3 ch**, 3 dc in next ch; repeat from * to end of row, ending last repeat at **, 2 dc in last ch; turn.

Row 2: Ch 3 (counts as 1 dc), 1 dc in first dc, *1 dc in each of next 3 dc, dc3tog over next 3 dc, 1 dc in each of next 3 dc, 3 dc in next dc; repeat from * ending last repeat with 2 dc in tch; turn.

Rows 3-12: Repeat Row 2. (In last dc of Row 12,

switch to Color B to complete final yo. See photo above.)

Rows 13-24: Using Color B, repeat Row 2. (In last dc of Row 24, switch to Color C to complete final yo.)

Rows 25-36: Using Color C, repeat Row 2. (In last dc of Row 36, switch to Color D to complete final yo.)

Rows 37-48: Using Color D, repeat Row 2. (In last dc of Row 48, switch to Color E to complete final yo.)

Rows 49-60: Using Color E, repeat Row 2. (In last dc of Row 60, switch to Color F to complete final yo.)

Rows 61-72: Using Color F, repeat Row 2.

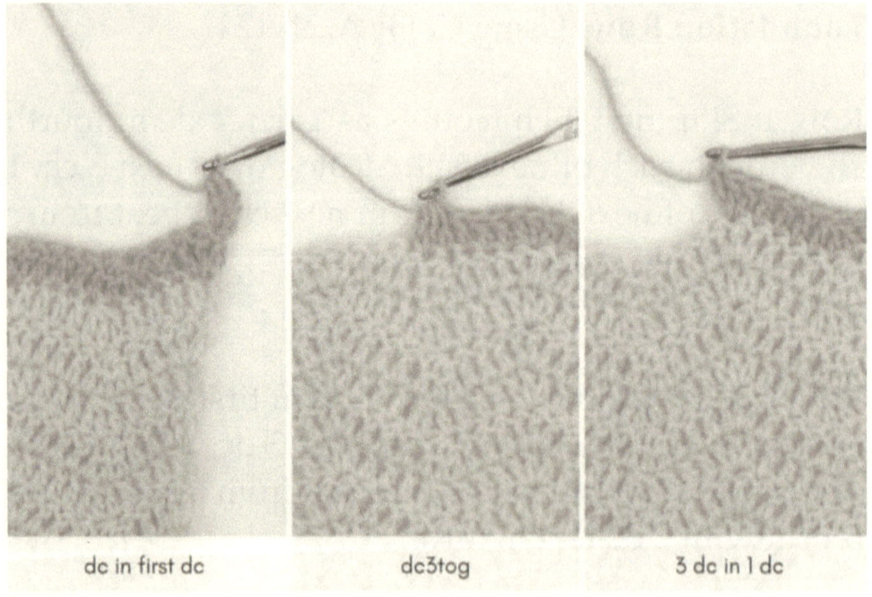

Fasten off and weave in any remaining ends.

Chunky Crochet Blanket Pattern

Grab some super bulky blanket yarn and crochet this v-stitch baby blanket!

HOW TO MAKE
Materials:

- 3 balls of Blanket Yarn
- L hook

Finished Blanket Measures: 40 x 42 inches

Instructions:
slip knot and chain 72 (needs to be a multiple of 6)
Feel free to use a different kind of yarn if you like.

<u>Row 1:</u> In the 4th chain from hook place 2 dc
skip a chain, 2 dc in the next chain and continue in
every chain going down.
Once you reach the end, 1 dc in the last chain
Ch 3 and turn

<u>Row 2:</u> 1dc in first stitch, skip 1 stitch, 2 dc in the next
stitch and repeat (the 2 dc should be in between the
"v" stitches front the first row) in the top chain on the
end, place 1 dc. ch 3 and turn

<u>Row 3:</u> Repeat until you use up 2 balls of yarn. Begin
using the 3rd ball, but only use about a 1/4 to leave
enough yarn for the border.

The Border

Once you finish crocheting the main body of the blanket, do not fasten off. Begin to sc down the left side of the blanket all the way down. If the stitches are "pulling" you have too few, if they are "rippling" you have too many. Make sure the sc stitches are laying flat.

Add 3sc in the 4 corners and complete all 4 sides. Try to make sure there are a similar number of stitches on the opposite sides. End the sc border round with a slip stitch.

sc in the next stitch, ch 2, sc in the same stitch (creates

a small shell). Continue this all the way around the edge and slip stitch to finish, weave in ends.

Triangle Patterned Granny Blankie

This pattern takes the classic granny stitch crochet motif and transforms it into a contemporary triangle baby blanket! This easy pattern keeps it interesting with the color changes that form the design.

HOW TO MAKE
SUPPLIES

- 2 skeins each of Lion Brand Vanna's Choice in Fisherman, Linen, Mustard, Taupe and Dark Grey Heather
- 1 Clover USA crochet hook J/6.00mm*
- scissors
- tapestry needle
- Modular Bobbin Holder

ABBREVIATIONS

- ch – chain stitch
- dc – double crochet

- sp (space) – indicates space between the 3dc clusters.
- sk – skip st. Do not work a chain over the skipped stitch.
- gr st (granny stitch) – Work 3 dc in space between the 3dc clusters from previous row.

PATTERN NOTES
- Skill level Easy.
- Gauge: Each 3 dc cluster is approximately 3/4 in square.
- You can cut bobbins for each triangle, or have multiple skeins in active use. One method to figure out the yarn needed for a bobbin is to measure the amount of yarn needed for a single granny stitch, then multiply that by the number of granny stitches in any particular half or whole triangle, while leaving a large margin of error.

Row 1: (in FISHERMAN) Work 109 foundation dc. Turn.

Row 2: (in FISHERMAN) Ch 3. Work dc in same st. Work [sk 2, 3 dc in next st] 5x. (in MUSTARD) Work [sk 2, 3 dc in next st]. (in DARK GREY HEATHER) Work [sk 2, 3 dc in next st] 11x. (in LINEN) Work [sk 2, 3 dc in next st]. (in FISHERMAN) Work [sk 2, 3 dc in next st] 11x. (in TAUPE) Work [sk 2, 3 dc in next st]. (in FISHERMAN) Work [sk 2, 3 dc in next st] 5x.

Sk 2.Work 2 dc in last st. Turn.

Row 3: (in FISHERMAN) Ch 3. Work 5 gr st. (in TAUPE) Work 2 gr st. (in FISHERMAN) Work 10 gr st. (in LINEN) Work 2 gr st. (in DARK GREY HEATHER) Work 10 gr st. (in MUSTARD) Work 2 gr st. (in FISHERMAN) Work 5 gr st. Work 1 dc in 3rd ch of previous row. Turn.

Row 4: (in FISHERMAN) Ch 3. Work dc in same st. Work 4 gr st. (in MUSTARD) Work 3 gr st. (in DARK GREY HEATHER) Work 9 gr st. (in LINEN) Work 3 gr st. (in FISHERMAN) Work 9 gr st. (in TAUPE) Work 3 gr st. (in FISHERMAN) Work 4 gr st. Work 2 dc in last sp. Turn.

Row 5: (in FISHERMAN) Ch 3. Work 4 gr st. (in TAUPE) Work 4 gr st. (in FISHERMAN) Work 8 gr st. (in LINEN) Work 4 gr st. (in DARK GREY HEATHER) Work 8 gr st. (in MUSTARD) Work 4 gr st. (in FISHERMAN) Work 4 gr st. Work 1 dc in 3rd ch of previous row. Turn.

Row 6: (in FISHERMAN) Ch 3. Work dc in same st. Work 3 gr st. (in MUSTARD) Work 5 gr st. (in DARK GREY HEATHER) Work 7 gr st. (in LINEN) Work 5 gr st. (in FISHERMAN) Work 7 gr st. (in TAUPE) Work 5 gr st. (in FISHERMAN) Work 3 gr st. Work 2 dc in last sp. Turn.

Row 7: (in FISHERMAN) Ch 3. Work 3 gr st. (in TAUPE) Work 6 gr st. (in FISHERMAN) Work 6 gr st. (in LINEN) Work 6 gr st. (in DARK GREY HEATHER) Work 6 gr st. (in MUSTARD) Work 6 gr st. (in FISHERMAN) Work 3 gr st. Work 1 dc in 3rd ch of previous row. Turn.

Row 8: (in FISHERMAN) Ch 3. Work dc in same st. Work 2 gr st. (in MUSTARD) Work 7 gr st. (in DARK GREY HEATHER) Work 5 gr st. (in LINEN) Work 7 gr st. (in FISHERMAN) Work 5 gr st. (in TAUPE) Work 7 gr st. (in FISHERMAN) Work 2 gr st. Work 2 dc in last sp. Turn.

Row 9: (in FISHERMAN) Ch 3. Work 2 gr st. (in TAUPE) Work 8 gr st. (in FISHERMAN) Work 4 gr st. (in LINEN) Work 8 gr st. (in DARK GREY HEATHER) Work 4 gr st. (in MUSTARD) Work 8 gr st. (in FISHERMAN) Work 2 gr st. Work 1 dc in 3rd ch of previous row. Turn.

Row 10: (in FISHERMAN) Ch 3. Work dc in same st. Work 1 gr st. (in MUSTARD) Work 9 gr st. (in DARK GREY HEATHER) Work 3 gr st. (in LINEN) Work 9 gr st. (in FISHERMAN) Work 3 gr st. (in TAUPE) Work 9 gr st. (in FISHERMAN) Work 1 gr st. Work 2 dc in last sp. Turn.

Row 11: (in FISHERMAN) Ch 3. Work 1 gr st. (in TAUPE) Work 10 gr st. (in FISHERMAN) Work 2 gr st. (in LINEN) Work 10 gr st. (in DARK GREY HEATHER) Work 2 gr st. (in MUSTARD) Work 10 gr st. (in FISHERMAN) Work 1 gr st. Work 1 dc in 3rd ch of previous row. Turn.

Row 12: (in FISHERMAN) Ch 3. Work dc in same st. (in MUSTARD) Work 11 gr st. (in DARK GREY HEATHER) Work 1 gr st. (in LINEN) Work 11 gr st. (in FISHERMAN) Work 1 gr st. (in TAUPE) Work 11 gr st. (in FISHERMAN) Work 2 dc in last sp. Turn.

Row 13: (in FISHERMAN) Ch 3. (in TAUPE) Work 12 gr st. (in LINEN) Work 12 gr st. (in MUSTARD) Work 12 gr st. (in FISHERMAN) Work 1 dc in 3rd ch of previous row. Turn.

Row 14: (in FISHERMAN) Ch 3. Work dc in same st. (in DARK GREY HEATHER) Work 11 gr st. (in TAUPE) Work 1 gr st. (in FISHERMAN) Work 11 gr st. (in DARK GREY HEATHER) Work 1 gr st. (in MUSTARD) Work 11 gr st. (in LINEN) Work 2 dc in last sp. Turn.

Row 15: (in LINEN) Ch 3. Work 1 gr st. (in MUSTARD) Work 10 gr st. (in DARK GREY HEATHER) Work 2 gr st. (in FISHERMAN) Work 10 gr st. (in TAUPE) Work 2 gr st. (in DARK GREY HEATHER) Work 10 gr st. (in FISHERMAN) Work 1 gr st. Work 1 dc in 3rd ch of previous row. Turn.

Row 16: (in FISHERMAN) Ch 3. Work dc in same st. Work 1 gr st. (in DARK GREY HEATHER) Work 9 gr st. (in TAUPE) Work 3 gr st. (in FISHERMAN) Work 9 gr st. (in DARK GREY HEATHER) Work 3 gr st. (in MUSTARD) Work 9 gr st. (in LINEN) Work 1 gr st. Work 2 dc in last sp. Turn.

Row 17: (in LINEN) Ch 3. Work 2 gr st. (in MUSTARD) Work 8 gr st. (in DARK GREY HEATHER) Work 4 gr st. (in FISHERMAN) Work 8 gr st. (in TAUPE) Work 4 gr st. (in DARK GREY HEATHER) Work 8 gr st. (in FISHERMAN) Work 2 gr st. Work 1 dc in 3rd ch of previous row. Turn.

Row 18: (in FISHERMAN) Ch 3. Work dc in same st. Work 2 gr st. (in DARK GREY HEATHER) Work 7 gr st. (in TAUPE) Work 5 gr st. (in FISHERMAN) Work 7 gr st. (in DARK GREY HEATHER) Work 5 gr st. (in MUSTARD) Work 7 gr st. (in LINEN) Work 2 gr st. Work 2 dc in last sp. Turn.

Row 19: (in LINEN) Ch 3. Work 3 gr st. (in MUSTARD) Work 6 gr st. (in DARK GREY HEATHER) Work 6 gr st. (in FISHERMAN) Work 6 gr st. (in TAUPE) Work 6 gr st. (in DARK GREY HEATHER) Work 6 gr st. (in FISHERMAN) Work 3 gr st. Work 1 dc in 3rd ch of previous row. Turn.

Row 20: (in FISHERMAN) Ch 3. Work dc in same st. Work 3 gr st. (in DARK GREY HEATHER) Work 5 gr st. (in TAUPE) Work 7 gr st. (in FISHERMAN) Work 5 gr st. (in DARK GREY HEATHER) Work 7 gr st. (in MUSTARD) Work 5 gr st. (in LINEN) Work 3 gr st. Work 2 dc in last sp. Turn.

Row 21: (in LINEN) Ch 3. Work 4 gr st. (in MUSTARD) Work 4 gr st. (in DARK GREY HEATHER) Work 8 gr st. (in FISHERMAN) Work 4 gr st. (in TAUPE) Work 8 gr st. (in DARK GREY HEATHER) Work 4 gr st. (in FISHERMAN) Work 4 gr st. Work 1 dc in 3rd ch of previous row. Turn.

Row 22: (in FISHERMAN) Ch 3. Work dc in same st. Work 4 gr st. (in DARK GREY HEATHER) Work 3 gr st. (in TAUPE) Work 9 gr st. (in FISHERMAN) Work 3 gr st. (in DARK GREY HEATHER) Work 9 gr st. (in MUSTARD) Work 3 gr st. (in LINEN) Work 4 gr st. Work 2 dc in last sp. Turn.

Row 23: (in LINEN) Ch 3. Work 5 gr st. (in MUSTARD) Work 2 gr st. (in DARK GREY HEATHER) Work 10 gr st. (in FISHERMAN) Work 2 gr st. (in TAUPE) Work 10 gr st. (in DARK GREY HEATHER) Work 2 gr st. (in FISHERMAN) Work 5 gr st. Work 1 dc in 3rd ch of previous row. Turn.

Row 24: (in FISHERMAN) Ch 3. Work dc in same st. Work 5 gr st. (in DARK GREY HEATHER) Work 1 gr st. (in TAUPE) Work 11 gr st. (in FISHERMAN) Work 1 gr st. (in DARK GREY HEATHER) Work 11 gr st.

(in MUSTARD) Work 1 gr st. (in LINEN) Work 5 gr st. Work 2 dc in last sp. Turn.

Row 25: (in LINEN) Ch 3. Work 6 gr st. (in DARK GREY HEATHER) Work 12 gr st. (in TAUPE) Work 12 gr st. (in FISHERMAN) Work 6 gr st. Work 1 dc in 3rd ch of previous row. Turn.

Row 26-49: Repeat Rows 2-25, changing colors as indicated by the graph. For Row 26, replace [sk 2, 3 dc in next st] with the 'gr st'.

Row 50-72: Repeat Rows 26-48, changing colors as indicated by the graph. (For Row 72, the widest triangle is 11 gr st across.)

Row 73: (in FISHERMAN) Ch 3. Work 1 dc in each st across. Fasten off.
All done!

Simple Stripe Textured Baby Blanket

This striped blankie uses a special double crochet two together stitch that creates a fantastic texture — without decreasing any stitches! Not only does this let you combine several colors to match the nursery decor, but it's also a good way to use single skeins that might be leftover from another project.

HOW TO MAKE
Materials:
- 6 skeins of Paintbox Yarn (I used 2 skeins of

Washed Teal, 2 skeins of Paper White, 1 skein of Slate Gray, and 1 skein of Spearmint Green). If you'd like to use a different yarn, you're going to need approximately 205 yards for each block of color or 1230 yards for the entire blanket.

- J Crochet Hook
- Tapestry Needle & Scissors

Pattern Notes:

- This pattern is worked through both loops.
- You do not work into the turning chain at the end of each row
- To make this pattern larger: increase your starting chain to the desired width. This pattern works with any chain length. Then, work until the blanket has reached your desired length. If your blanket is much wider than mine, you'll want to use two skeins of each yarn for each color block.
- dc2tog stitches are all worked in the same stitch for this pattern

Special Stitch:

dc2tog: yarn over, insert yarn into stitch, pull up a loop. Pull through two loops. Yarn over, insert hook into same stitch, pull up a loop. Pull through two loops. Pull through 3 loops
Ch 72.

Row 1: dc in the third chain from hook. dc2tog in each stitch across. Ch 2, turn. (You should have 1 dc and 69 dc2tog).

Rows 2-11: dc in the first stitch, dc2tog in each stitch across. Do NOT work into the turning chain in this row or any other. Ch 2, turn.

Row 12: dc in the first stitch, dc2tog in each stitch across. Cut yarn, and weave ends.

Row 13: Join yarn using your preferred method. Ch 2. dc in the first stitch, dc2tog in each stitch across. Ch 2, turn.

Rows 14-23: dc in the first stitch, dc2tog in each stitch across. Ch 2, turn.

Row 24: dc in the first stitch, dc2tog in each stitch across. Cut yarn and weave ends.

Continue working 12 rows of each color until you reach your desired length. My blanket is 72 rows long (6 color changes).

Fast and Easy Moss Stitch Baby Blanket

Once you learn the simple pattern for this soft baby blanket, you'll be able to crochet away while you chat with a friend or watch a favorite movie. If you can chain and single crochet, you can make this blanket.

HOW TO MAKE
What You'll Need
Equipment / Tools:
- Crochet hook
- Tapestry needle
- Stitch marker

Materials: Bernat Softee baby yarn

Instructions
Yarn Information

The recommended yarn for this project is Bernat Softee baby yarn. The weight is "light worsted," "DK," or "Double Knitting." This is important to know in case you want to select a different yarn to substitute; look for the same weight if you aim to create a blanket with the same drape. That said, you can use any yarn weight and a corresponding hook size to create an easy crochet baby blanket using this pattern.

Blanket Sizes: Preemie, Newborn, Toddler
This crochet baby blanket pattern includes instructions for three sizes: preemie, newborn, and toddler. Instructions list the smallest size first with changes for the larger sizes noted in parentheses.

The measurements below don't include any edging; if you wish to add a baby blanket edging, your finished blanket will be a little bit bigger.
- Preemie: The smallest blanket measures about 26 inches wide by 34 inches long. If you crochet your blanket using Bernat Softee, you will need two to three 5-oz skeins of yarn to complete this project, depending on how tight you crochet. As far as yardage goes, you'll need about 724 yards/662 meters for the blanket itself, plus a bit more for your gauge swatch.
- Newborn/receiving blanket: The mid-sized blanket is 30 inches square. You can make it a little bit longer if you prefer a more rectangular

shape for the blanket. If so, aim for 30" x 34". You will need two to three of the 5-oz balls of Bernat Softee for this size, depending on how tight you crochet.

- Toddler: The largest of the blankets measures 36 inches by 44 inches. You will need four 5-oz balls of Bernat Softee to crochet this size.

Abbreviations Used in This Pattern
- ch = chain
- ch-1 sp = chain-1 space, the space formed when you crochet a chain stitch in the previous row
- rep = repeat
- sc = single crochet
- st = stitch

Gauge
- Stitch gauge: 4 stitches = 1 inch when crocheting the stitch pattern as instructed below.
- Row gauge: The row gauge is not important for this pattern.

Crochet a Gauge Swatch
To check your gauge, crochet a gauge swatch. Form a starting chain of 25 stitches and crochet using the blanket pattern instructions until your piece is square. End off. Measure your swatch to see how many stitches per inch you are crocheting. Compare your gauge against that recommended in the pattern

(above). If you are crocheting fewer stitches per inch than recommended, try again with a smaller crochet hook. If you are crocheting more stitches per inch, try again with a larger hook.

The swatching process is necessary because you want your baby blanket to be a useable size. If your gauge is different, your baby blanket could finish at the wrong size or you may run out of yarn before finishing the blanket.

Design Notes

The pattern directions instruct you to crochet into the ch-1 spaces. If you have difficulty finding these — sometimes they seem to vanish — carefully poke your finger at the row of stitches from back to front. Your hands will feel the gap even if your eyes don't spot it at first.

How to Crochet a Baby Blanket

- **Begin Row One**

Ch 105 (121, 145). Remember, the instructions are for the small size (with the medium, large in the parenthesis). Place a stitch marker in the first ch from your hook. Sc in 3rd ch from hook. [ch 1, skip next ch, sc in next ch.] Rep across the entire row. ch 1, turn.

- **Start on Row Two**

[sc in the next ch-1 sp, ch 1.] Rep the sequence in brackets across the rest of the row. At the end of the row, work a sc st into the st where you placed the marker; you can remove the marker before working the stitch. ch 1, turn.

- **Continue Rows Three and Up**

The rest of the rows are all exactly the same as row 2, with one minor difference: at the end of the row, work your last sc st into the turning chain of the previous row. Rep this row until the baby blanket reaches your desired length.

- **Finish Off Your Blanket**

When the baby blanket is the length that you want, cut the yarn, leaving at least six inches of extra yarn. Thread the tapestry needle with the yarn end and use the needle to weave the loose end of the yarn into the blanket. Repeat with any other loose ends you may have hanging from the blanket (which occur when you switch from one ball of yarn to the next).

This crochet pattern works fine without any additional edging, but you can add an edging if you want to. There are many baby blanket edgings to choose from. A simple single crochet stitch around the entire edge of the blanket is an easy choice that goes well with the single crochet design in this pattern.

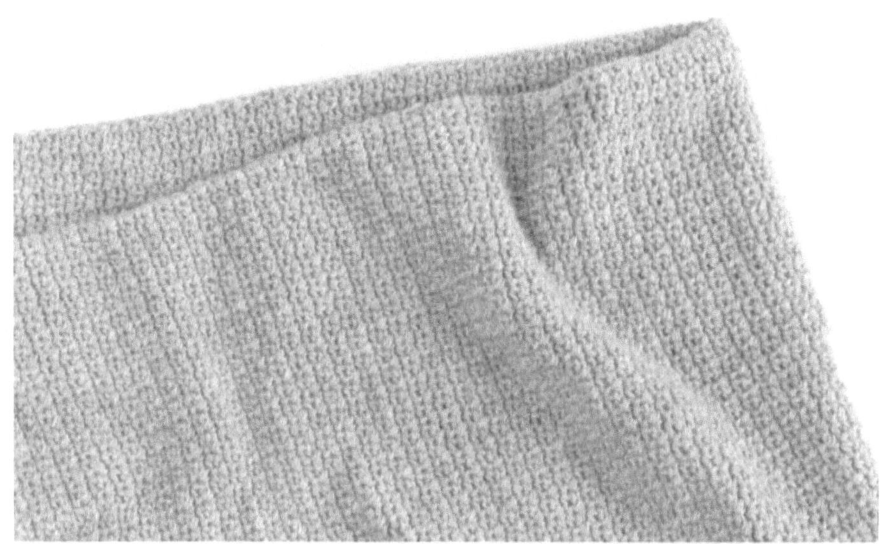

Colorful Round Blanket Pattern

Crochet this gorgeous blanket in the round for a less expected shape! It might look complicated with all those ripples and colors, but you won't need to change colors at all. Because the yarn takes care of that for you. And the rounds themselves use shell stitches and double crochet, so it's perfect anyone with minimal crochet experience.

HOW TO MAKE
SIZE
About 43 in. (109 cm) across, at widest

MATERIALS
- Lion Brand® Mandala® Baby (Art. #526)
- 207 Honey Dukes 2 balls

- Lion Brand® crochet hook size H-8 (5 mm)
- Lion Brand® stitch markers
- Lion Brand® large-eyed blunt needle

GAUGE
Rnds 1-4 = about 4 in. (10 cm) diameter.

BE SURE TO CHECK YOUR GAUGE.

STITCH EXPLANATIONS
beg-Shell Ch 3 (counts as dc), (dc, ch 2, 2 dc) in indicated sp.

Shell Work (2 dc, ch 2, 2 dc) in indicated sp.

ABBREVIATIONS
beg = begin(ning)(s)
ch = chain
ch-sp(s) = chain space(s) previously made
dc = double crochet
rem = remain
rep = repeat
rnd(s) = round(s)
RS = right side
sc in single crochet
sk = skip
sl st = slip stitch
st(s) = stitch(es)

<u>**NOTES**</u>
1. Blankie is worked in joined rnds in a ripple pattern with RS always facing.
2. The ripple pattern is easy to do, but it's important to remember that you may need to work several rnds before the ripple pattern becomes clear.
3. The ripple pattern consists of alternating peaks and valleys. Peaks are formed by working a Shell in the ch-2 sp of the Shells in the previous rnd. Valleys are formed by skipping sts centered between two peaks.
4. Beg in Rnd 6, stitch markers are used to mark valleys. If you are comfortable "reading" your stitches, you may choose not to use the markers.
5. For those who find visuals helpful, we have included stitch diagrams.

BLANKIE

Ch 5; join with sl st in first ch to make a ring.

Rnd 1 (RS): Ch 3 (counts as dc), work 11 more dc in ring; join with sl st in top of beg ch-3 – you will have 12 dc in this rnd.

Rnd 2: Ch 4 (counts as dc, ch 1), dc in next st, *ch 1, dc in next st; rep from * around, ch 1; join with sl st in 3rd ch of beg ch-4 – 12 dc and 12 ch-1 sps.

Rnd 3: Sl st in first ch-1 sp, ch 5 (counts as dc, ch 2), dc in same ch-1 sp, (dc, ch 2, dc) in each rem ch-1 sp around; join with sl st in 3rd ch of beg ch-5 – 24 dc and 12 ch-2 sps.

Rnd 4: Sl st in first ch-2 sp, beg-Shell in same ch-2 sp, Shell in each rem ch-2 sp around; join with sl st in top of beg ch-3 – 12 Shells (counting dc sts in Shells – for a total of 48 dc and 12 ch-2 sps).

Rnd 5: Sl st in next dc, ch 3 (counts as dc), Shell in ch-2 sp of first Shell, dc in next st, *sk next 2 sts, dc in next st, Shell in ch-2 sp of next Shell, dc in next st; rep from * around; join with sl st in top of beg ch-3 – 12 Shells and 24 dc (for a total 72 dc and 12 ch-2 sps).

Rnd 6: Sl st in next dc, ch 3 (counts as dc), dc in next st, Shell in ch-2 sp of first Shell, dc in next 2 sts, place a marker in last dc made, *sk next 2 sts, dc in next 2 sts, Shell in ch-2 sp of next Shell, dc in next 2 sts, place a marker in last dc made; rep from * around; join with sl st in top of beg ch-3 – 12 Shells and 48 dc (for a total of 96 dc and 12 ch-2 sps).

Rnd 7: Sl st in next 2 dc, ch 3 (counts as dc), dc in each st to ch-2 sp of first Shell, Shell in ch-2 sp, dc in each st to 1 st before first marked dc, *sk next 4 sts, move marker to last dc made, dc in each st to ch-2 sp of next Shell, Shell in ch-2 sp, dc in each st to 1 st before next marked dc; rep from * around, move marker to last dc made; join with sl st in top of beg ch-3.

Rnds 8 and 9: Sl st in next dc, ch 3 (counts as dc), dc in each st to ch-2 sp of first Shell, Shell in ch-2 sp, dc in each st to first marked dc, *sk marked dc and next dc, move marker to last dc made, dc in each st to ch-2 sp of next Shell, Shell in ch-2 sp, dc in each st to next marked dc; rep from * around, move marker to last dc made; join with sl st in top of beg ch-3 – 12 Shells and 96 dc (for a total of 144 dc and 12 ch-2 sps; 6 dc along each of 24 edges, between ch-2 sp peaks and skipped st valleys) in Rnd 9.

Rnds 10-33: Rep Rnds 7-9 for 8 more times – 12 Shells and 528 dc (22 dc along each of 24 edges) in Rnd 33.

Rnd 34: (Sl st, ch 1, sc) in next dc, sc in each st to ch-2 sp of first Shell, 3 sc inch-2 sp, sc in each st to marked dc, *sk marked dc and next dc, remove marker, sc in each st to ch-2 sp of next Shell, 3 sc in ch-2 sp, sc in each st to next marked dc; rep from * around, remove marker; join with sl st in first sc – 540 sc (22 sc along each of 24 edges between peaks (center sc of 3-sc groups) and skipped st valleys).
Fasten off.

FINISHING

Weave in ends.

Basketweave Crochet Baby Blanket Pattern

Basketweave crochet is a beautiful textured stitch that is easy to make once you've learned how to crochet post stitches. It is perfect for baby blankets because it is thick, cozy, and warm. More importantly, it is dense, without holes between the stitches for the baby's fingers and toes to get caught up in.

<table><tr><td>

Tip

The idea behind this tutorial is to provide information that helps you to make your own baby blanket design, which means that the materials you choose to use are entirely up to you! You can use lightweight yarn and a small crochet hook, bulky yarn and a large crochet hook, or anything in between.

</td></tr></table>

Basics of Basketweave Stitch

Basketweave crochet stitch is created using both front and back post stitches. Double crochet post stitches are most common, but you can create this stitch in half double crochet, treble, and taller post stitches if you desire. The basketweave design is created by alternating sections of front post stitches with sections of back post stitches. A common choice is to make five front post stitches followed by five back post stitches across the row. However, you can do fewer or more as you prefer.

The key to basketweave stitch is that after a certain number of rows, you reverse the pattern—working back post stitches into the front post stitches and front post stitches into the back post stitches. You can alternate after any number of rows you want, although it is common to switch after the same number as the number used across; if you crocheted five front post and five back post across, then you'll also crochet five rows before reversing. This is what gives the most even, checkerboard feel to basketweave crochet.

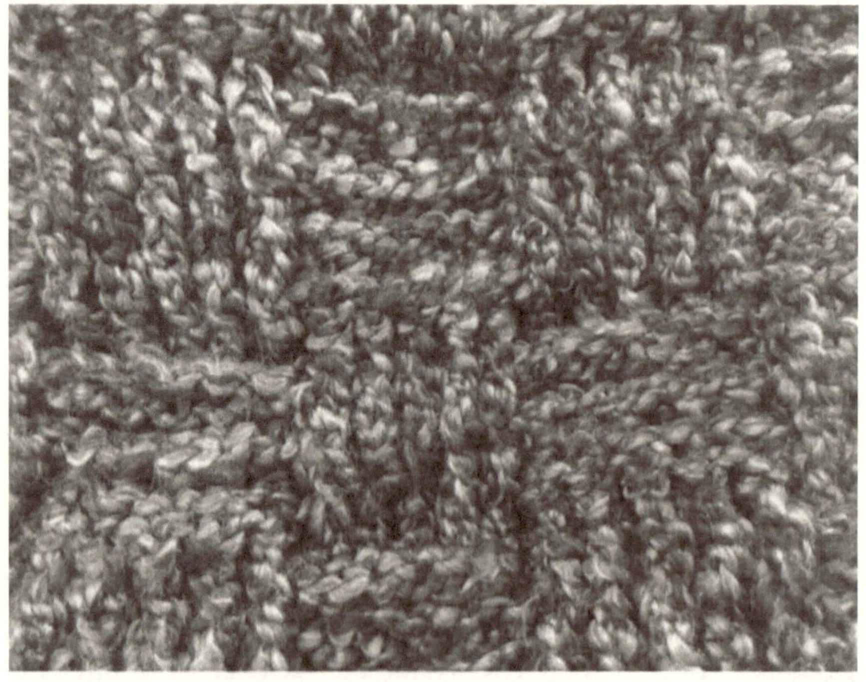

What You'll Need

Equipment / Tools: 1 Size N crochet hook
Materials

- 3 colors bulky-weight yarn (one skein each)
- 1 color novelty yarn

Instructions

1. Choose the Blanket Size

You can make your blanket any size you wish, of course. When you look at standard bed and blanket sizes, you'll see that crib blankets are typically 45 x 60 inches, although daily use blankets are much smaller — around 26 x 34 inches for preemies and up to 36 x 44 inches for toddlers. Square baby blankets are common and may be as small as 18-inches-square for preemies or as large as twice that for other young babies. The great thing about crochet baby blankets is that the size really doesn't have to be exact.

2. Start Your Foundation Chain

Crochet a chain that is slightly shorter than your desired blanket width. Your foundation row needs to have enough chains to accommodate your choice, so if you're going to crochet five of each stitch, make sure you begin with a chain that is a multiple of five plus the number needed for your turning chain (three if you are using double crochet).

3. Row One

Crochet your chosen stitch into each stitch across. So, if you are using double crochet, make one double crochet in each stitch across the row.

4. Row Two

Now you begin your post stitches. Begin with your turning chain. Alternate front and back post double crochet stitches across the row in groups; for example, 5 front post double crochet, five back post double crochet across the row. You may wish to end with a double crochet stitch in the top of the final stitch for a more even edge.

5. Next Group of Rows

Crochet several rows (four more if you want to do rows of five before reversing). Each row will alternate whether you begin with fpdc or bpdc (because you are turning the work you must work back into front and front into back so that the stitches always protrude out on the same side).

6. Reverse Direction, First Row

When you've completed a set of rows, you are ready to reverse direction. Now you will want to crochet the opposite way so that the texture of your post stitches protrudes in the opposite direction. In this instance, you are going to crochet the same stitch into each stitch (instead of working a front post into a back post as before, you are going to work a front post into a front post—becauseyou have turned the work, this results in opposite-facing textures).

7. Next Group of Rows

After you've crocheted the first new row, go back to before, alternating so that you work front posts into back posts. You'll continue working rows, reversing direction every few rows (five if you're following our pattern) to the end of the project.

> **Tip**
>
> One of the choices that you get to make to customize this baby blanket is to crochet it in different colors. You can use the same color throughout or change as many times as you want. Feel free to choose whatever color changes feel right for your baby blanket.

8. Add a Border

Continue your basketweave crochet pattern until your baby blanket has reached almost the desired final length. End off with a slip stitch. Now you can add any border of your choosing to the blanket to give it a finished look. A single crochet edge of novelty yarn is a nice choice.

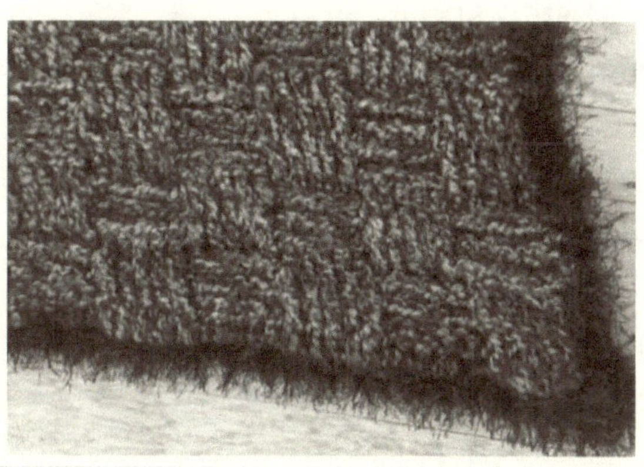

Step-By-Step Instructions

You have all of the information that you need to crochet your own basketweave baby blanket design. But if you're working on the blanket for your first time, it might help to have a step-by-step pattern.

1. Chain 63. Double crochet in the fourth chain from hook. Double chain in each stitch across (Total 60 double chain).
2. Chain three, turn. Five front post double crochet, five back post double crochet across row ending with a double crochet in top of the last stitch.
3. Chain three, turn. Five back post double crochet, five front post double crochet across row ending with a double crochet in top of last stitch.
4. Repeat steps two and three one time.
5. Repeat step two twice. (The second time reverses the direction and begins the second section of basketweave crochet.)
6. Repeat step three, then step two.
7. Repeat step six.
8. Repeat step four twice.
9. Repeat step five.
10. Repeat step six twice.
11. Change color.
12. Repeat steps eight through 10.
13. Change color.
14. Repeat step 12 two times.

15.Finish off, weave in ends.
16.Join novelty yarn in any color. Chain one.
   Single crochet in each stitch all the way around.
   Slip stitch to join to chain one. Finish off and
   weave in ends.